Simran Makes a Splash

by Ian MacDonald

illustrated by Robin Boyden

It is Simran's birthday!

"We are off to Splash Park," says Mum.

Mum packs two bags.

On the bus, Simran can hardly wait!

“Would you like a birthday treat?” asks Mum.

Simran picks a stingray swim ring.

Mum places the bags neatly into lockers.

"Where shall we start?" she asks.

"The main pool," says Simran.

When they arrive, the pool looks big!
Noisy children play in the waves.

Simran and Mum walk into the water.

“Stay near me,” says Mum.

Simran splashes and kicks her legs.

"Your stingray ring helps you float," says Mum.

“What are those two big tubes?” asks Simran.

“Those are the flumes. Shall we have a go?” replies Mum.

“Put your ring at the side,” says Mum.

“I’ll ride first, then you come next,” says Mum.

Simran feels daunted waiting at the red light.

The green light comes on. Water sprays as Simran races down the flume.

“I have got you!” Mum exclaims.

Next, Simran and Mum go to the play pool.
Jets of water shoot out and buckets tip.

A helper in a red shirt smiles at Simran.
Simran smiles and waves back.

Simran and Mum go back to the main pool. The foaming water swirls and spins.

"Look out, Simran," calls Mum. "The water in that stream is very fast!"

Oh no! The stingray ring slips away. Simran tries to swim after it.

“That stream is unsafe for you, Simran,” Mum says.

Simran looks sadly at her stingray ring. It is swept away into the rushing foam.

Mum gets milkshakes. A tear trickles down Simran's cheek.

"Where could Stinger be?" Simran says sadly.

Then the helper in the red shirt appears.

“Is this yours?” she asks.

Under her arm is Simran’s stingray ring.

“Hooray!” shouts Simran. “Thank you for bringing back Stinger.”

Look Back

Encourage students to use the map of the water park to retell the story.